Flying machines

Peter Firmin

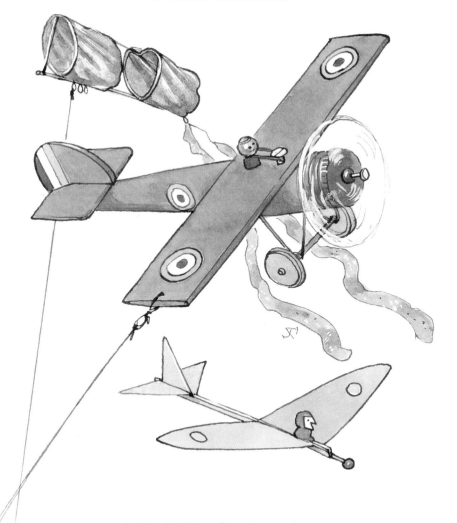

A & C Black · London

Contents

With grateful thanks to the following people who helped to make the models for this book: Dorian, Lewis, Ruth, Olivia, Sam, Laurence and Oliver.

A CIP catalogue record for this book is available from the British Library.

First published 1994 by A & C Black (Publishers) Ltd
35 Bedford Row, London WC1R 4JH

ISBN 0-7136-3622-X

© 1994 A & C Black (Publishers) Ltd

Filmset by Rowland Phototypesetting Limited
Bury St Edmunds, Suffolk.
Printed in Great Britain by
Cambus Litho Limited, East Kilbride.

About this book

In this book, there are detailed instructions to help you make darts, gliders, kites and many other working models. Once you have made some darts, gliders and kites try to make the more complicated models such as the Gypsy Moth biplane and the Red Baron's triplane. Although these planes are too small and heavy to glide, you can have fun flying them on a string.

Before you begin, take time to read the instructions for the models carefully. Look at the illustrations, too, before you set to work. Some of the models will take time to make, so don't try and do everything in one go.

On page 5 there's a list of things you will need. It's a good idea to have two large boxes to put everything in – one for all your materials and one for your tools. Most of the materials you will need are things you can find around the house; things which would normally be thrown away.

You will need to buy some materials, such as PVA glue and wire. But you can save money by sharing these and your tools with friends.

I hope you'll have fun making and using these models. Why not try inventing and making some models of your own?

Glossary

This glossary explains some of the words used in this book and describes the various parts used to make the models. All words in the glossary appear in the text in **bold** type.

Aerofoil section   the cross-section of a wing, **tailplane** or **fin** which affects its flight.

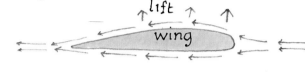

Biplane   an aeroplane with two main wings.

Bridle   the strings attached to a kite to which the flying line is fixed.

Drag   the wind resistance of any part of a glider, aeroplane or kite.

Equilateral triangle   a triangle with three equal sides.

Fin   the upright part of a tail.

Gravity   the pull of an object towards the Earth.

What brought you down to earth?

gravity!

Impetus   the force that keeps something moving.

Lift   the shape of a wing gives the aeroplane lift to help it rise into the air.

Monoplane a plane with only one main wing.

Plane   a wing or level surface which supports flight.

Spine   the central pole of a kite or glider to which the other parts are fixed.

Tailplane   the small level wing at the back of an aeroplane or glider.

Triplane   an aeroplane with three main wings.

That was a triplane, that was.

Windsock   a tube of cloth flown on a pole to show the direction of the wind.

Tools, equipment . . .

awl for making holes
block of wood
brushes
bulldog clips and pegs
coloured paints
compasses
craft knife
hacksaw
hammer

hand drill
newspaper to work on
paperclips
pencil and ruler
pens
pliers
PVA glue
school glue
scissors

sponge for putting on paint
sticky tape
varnish
vice
white emulsion paint
wire cutters
wood glue

and materials

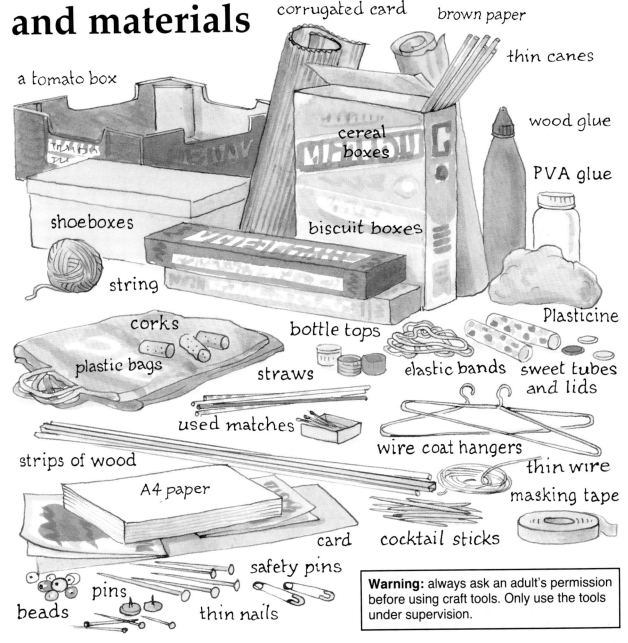

corrugated card

brown paper

thin canes

a tomato box

cereal boxes

wood glue

PVA glue

shoeboxes

biscuit boxes

string

Plasticine

corks

bottle tops

elastic bands

sweet tubes and lids

plastic bags

straws

used matches

wire coat hangers

strips of wood

thin wire

masking tape

A4 paper

card

cocktail sticks

beads

pins

safety pins

thin nails

Warning: always ask an adult's permission before using craft tools. Only use the tools under supervision.

Useful tips

Before you begin, read these pages carefully. They will tell you which tools to use for which jobs, and how to use them safely.

Paper

Use good quality paper to make the paper planes. Strong brown parcel paper is good for making kites. The paper needn't be new.

Cutting

Where possible, use scissors to cut card and boxes. The best sort have rounded ends. Never point scissors at anyone.

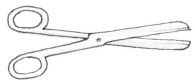

If you want to use a craft knife, ask an adult. Make sure the knife is sharp. Protect your work surface by cutting on to a thick pad of newspaper on top of a piece of card.

If you are cutting a box with a knife, put a block of wood inside the box so you've got a hard surface to press down on.

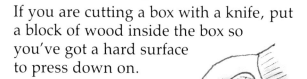

Gluing

Use small pegs or bulldog clips to hold glued pieces of card together. Use blocks of wood to keep things in place while the glue is drying. The joins can be made stronger with sticky tape.

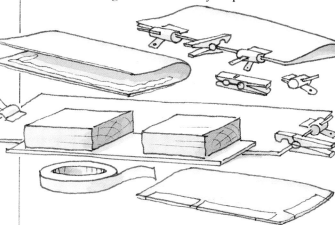

Making holes

Put a block of wood on top of your work surface so you've got a hard surface to press down on. Use an awl or a compass point to make the holes.

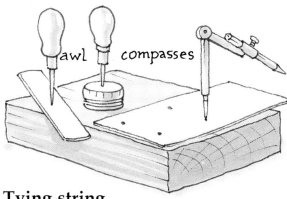

awl   compasses

Tying string

The best knot for tying string to canes or metal rings is a clove hitch. It is easy to tie and can be moved along the cane. Finish off with a half hitch.

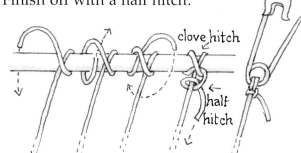

clove hitch

← half hitch

Cutting wire and wood

Use pliers to cut wire, thin cane and cocktail sticks.

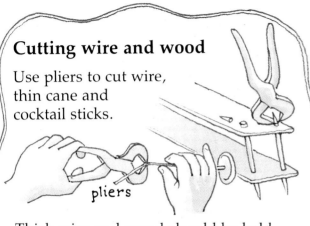

pliers

Thick wire and wood should be held securely in a vice and cut with a hacksaw. Keep your fingers clear of the saw.

hacksaw

vice

Drawing equilateral triangles

Draw a line 1cm from the bottom edge of a piece of card 16 × 30cm.

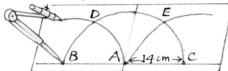

Place the compass point in the centre of this line at A. Draw a half circle with a radius of 14cm, and label points B and C. Place the compass point at B, and draw a part circle, as shown. Label point D. Place the compass point at C, and draw another part cicle. Label point E.

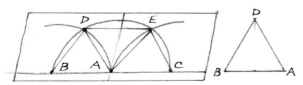

Join up points BD, DA, AE, EC and DE. Cut along the lines to make three **equilateral triangles**.

Bending card

If you want to bend a piece of card to get an even curve for a wing of a plane, it's best to score the card first. Draw several lines across the card where you want the curve to be.

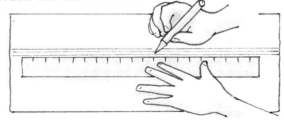

Place the edge of a metal ruler along one of the lines. Press down firmly and run the blunt point of a knitting needle down the card, following the edge of the ruler. Do the same along the other lines.

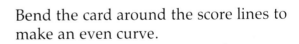

Bend the card around the score lines to make an even curve.

Hammering

Before hammering a nail into a piece of wood, drill a fine hole with a hand drill. This will stop the wood splitting.

hand drill

Kites

Kites were invented in China nearly 2000 years ago. Kites are usually flown for fun, but they can carry objects into space, such as a thermometer to measure the temperature of the air, or a camera to take aerial photographs.

To fly a kite successfully, you need to keep the kite pointing upwards and facing the wind, otherwise it is likely to move sideways, and dive and spin.

The angle of the kite to the wind is controlled by the position of the flying line or by the length of the strings of the **bridle**. The kite's tail adds weight and **drag** which also helps to keep the kite facing the wind.

You will find instructions for making a simple bag kite and a hexagonal kite on the next four pages.

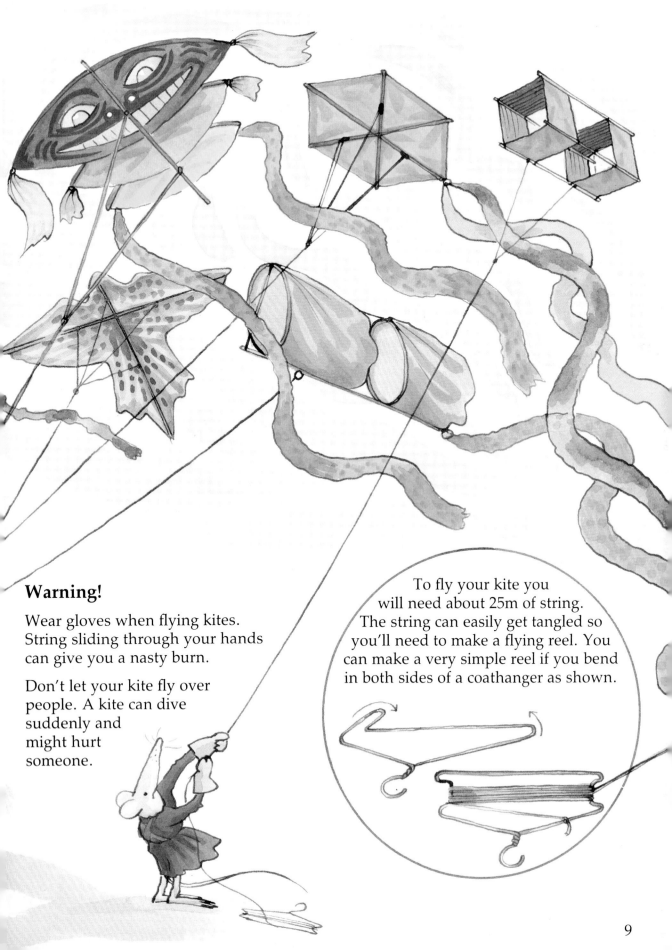

Warning!

Wear gloves when flying kites. String sliding through your hands can give you a nasty burn.

Don't let your kite fly over people. A kite can dive suddenly and might hurt someone.

To fly your kite you will need about 25m of string. The string can easily get tangled so you'll need to make a flying reel. You can make a very simple reel if you bend in both sides of a coathanger as shown.

A bag kite

You will need: 2 wire coathangers, a 75cm garden cane, 3 large thin plastic carrier bags, four 10cm lengths of thin wire, 1.5m of thin string, 25m of strong string and 2 safety pins.

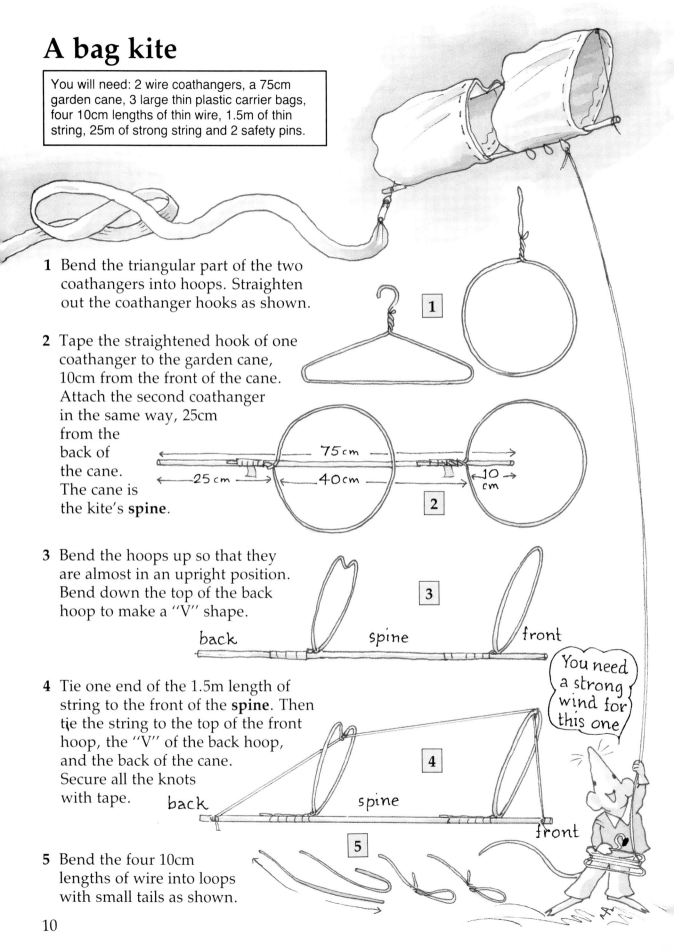

1 Bend the triangular part of the two coathangers into hoops. Straighten out the coathanger hooks as shown.

2 Tape the straightened hook of one coathanger to the garden cane, 10cm from the front of the cane. Attach the second coathanger in the same way, 25cm from the back of the cane. The cane is the kite's **spine**.

75cm

25cm   40cm   10 cm

3 Bend the hoops up so that they are almost in an upright position. Bend down the top of the back hoop to make a "V" shape.

back   spine   front

4 Tie one end of the 1.5m length of string to the front of the **spine**. Then tie the string to the top of the front hoop, the "V" of the back hoop, and the back of the cane. Secure all the knots with tape.

back   spine   front

You need a strong wind for this one

5 Bend the four 10cm lengths of wire into loops with small tails as shown.

10

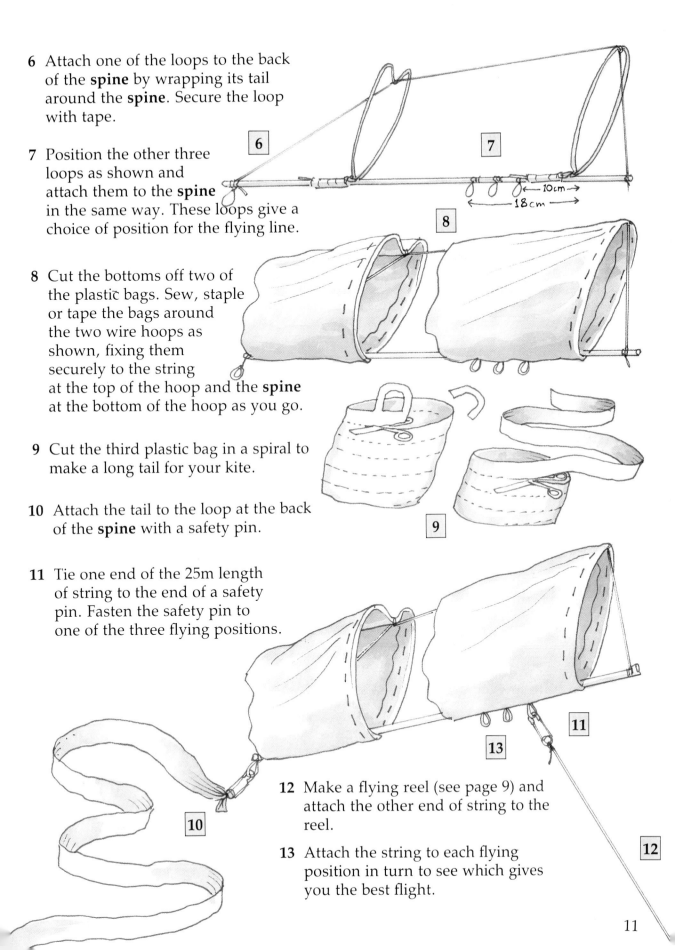

6 Attach one of the loops to the back of the **spine** by wrapping its tail around the **spine**. Secure the loop with tape.

7 Position the other three loops as shown and attach them to the **spine** in the same way. These loops give a choice of position for the flying line.

8 Cut the bottoms off two of the plastic bags. Sew, staple or tape the bags around the two wire hoops as shown, fixing them securely to the string at the top of the hoop and the **spine** at the bottom of the hoop as you go.

9 Cut the third plastic bag in a spiral to make a long tail for your kite.

10 Attach the tail to the loop at the back of the **spine** with a safety pin.

11 Tie one end of the 25m length of string to the end of a safety pin. Fasten the safety pin to one of the three flying positions.

12 Make a flying reel (see page 9) and attach the other end of string to the reel.

13 Attach the string to each flying position in turn to see which gives you the best flight.

10cm

18cm

A hexagonal kite

You will need: a sheet of strong parcel paper 70 × 80cm, three 75cm garden canes, one 20cm length and one 3m length of thin string, a plastic work surface, 10cm of thin wire, 2 strong safety pins, 2 plastic bags and one 160cm length, one 88cm length and one 25m length of strong string.

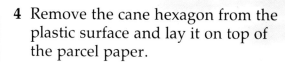

1 Mark the centre of each of the canes. Bind together the centre of the canes with the 20cm length of thin string. The canes are the ribs of the kite.

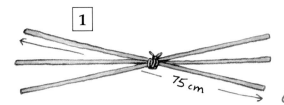

1

75 cm

2 Arrange the canes into a hexagonal shape on top of a plastic work surface. The canes should be equally spaced so that the distance between the end of each cane is the same. Tape the canes to the plastic work surface.

3 Tie one end of the 3m length of thin string to the end of one of the canes. Take the string around the edge of the cane structure, tying it to the ends of the canes as you go. Tape the string firmly to each cane.

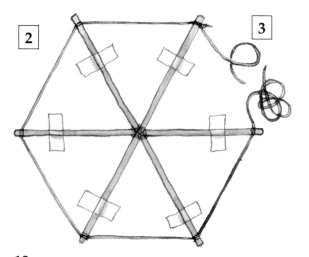

2

3

4 Remove the cane hexagon from the plastic surface and lay it on top of the parcel paper.

5 Draw round the outside of the cane hexagon leaving a 3cm gap all the way around. Remove the canes from the paper.

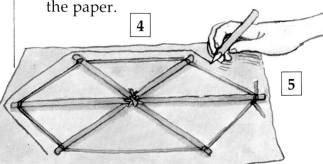

4

5

6 Cut out the hexagon shape from the paper. Turn each of the six corners over and glue them into position.

6

7 Lay the cane hexagon on top of the paper hexagon. Fold each of the sides over so that they cover the string outline. Glue and tape the folded paper into position.

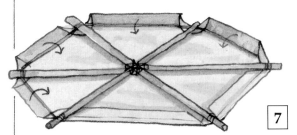

7

11 Tie one end of the string to rib 1 and the other end to rib 2 of the kite.

8 Turn the kite over and cut a 6cm slot along every other rib so that you can see the cane.
Tape around the slots to stop the paper tearing.

Cover the ends of each cane for safety.

9 Turn the kite over and tape the ribs to the back of the paper.

10 To make the **bridle**, tie a small loop in the centre of the 160cm length of strong string.

12 Tie one end of the 88cm length of strong string to rib 3 of the kite. Make a loop in the other end of the string.

rib 1

rib 3

rib 2

bridle

80 cm

72 cm

13 Tie a safety pin to one end of the 25m length of string. Fasten the safety pin to the two **bridle** loops.

14 Make a flying reel (see page 9) and attach the other end of the string to the reel.

15 Cut two plastic bags in spirals to make a double tail for your kite (see page 11).

16 Bend the 10cm length of wire into a loop with a small tail as shown. Attach the loop to the end of rib 3.

Move the flying reel from side to side to control the kite.

17 Attach the tail to the loop with a safety pin.

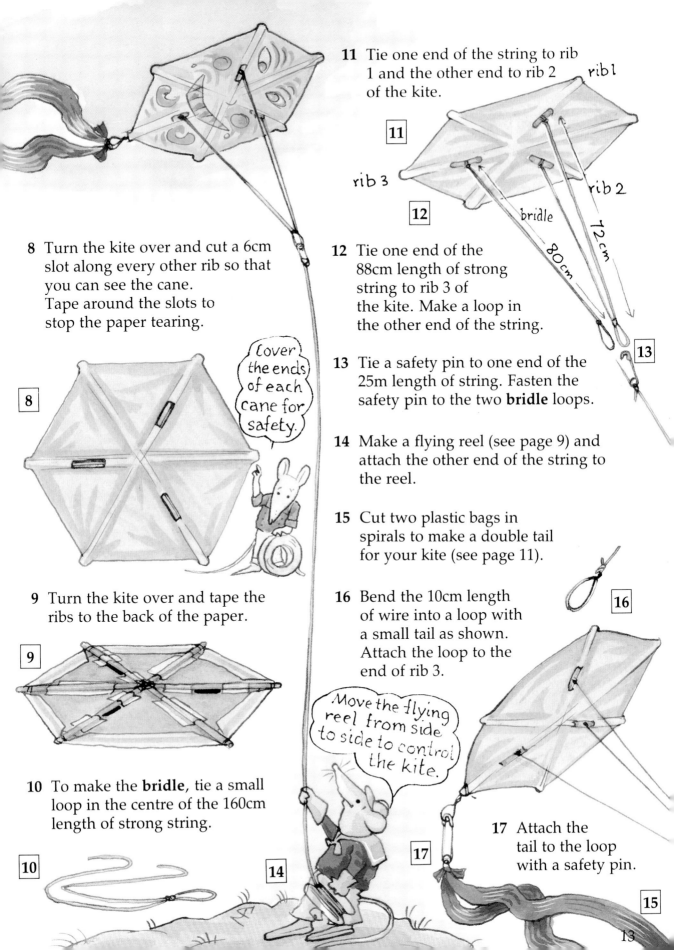

13

What makes a machine fly?

Three things are needed to make a flying machine overcome the force of **gravity** and rise into the air.

a the **lift** given by a **plane** or wing to make the machine rise.

b power to drive the machine through the air.

c the **drag** of a tail to keep the machine facing forward into the wind.

A paper dart

You will need: an A4 sheet of paper.

1 Fold the sheet of paper in half lengthways.

2 Fold the corners over at one end.

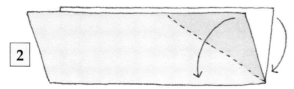

3 Fold the corners over again and glue them into position.

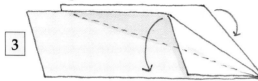

4 Fold the corners over again.

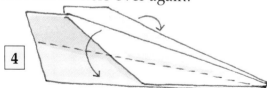

5 Throw the dart fast and straight for the best results.

The perfect paper plane

This paper plane is easy to make and its performance as a glider is almost perfect. You can make the plane loop the loop and spin by bending the tips of the wings and tail.

You will need: an A4 sheet of paper.

1 Fold and unfold one end of the paper to make two diagonal creases.

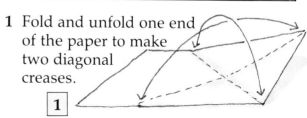

2 Mark A, B and C on the paper in the positions shown.

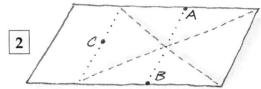

3 Pinch the paper so that A and B meet in the centre.

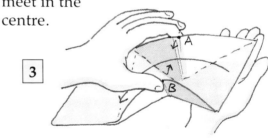

4 Keeping A and B together, bring them down to meet C. Press the paper flat to make a triangle.
Mark D, E and F on the paper in the positions shown.

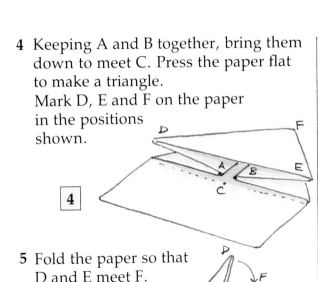

5 Fold the paper so that D and E meet F.

6 Make creases by folding and unfolding the paper along the dotted lines as shown.

7 Mark G and H on the paper in the positions shown.

8 Pinch point G from underneath and push the pinched part forward along the creases. Do the same at H. Press the paper flat as shown.

9 To make the tail, cut a strip, 4cm wide, from the end of the paper. Fold the strip in half lengthways.

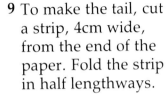
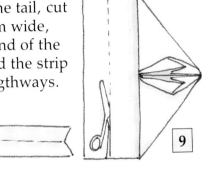

10 Fold the plane in half to make the wings. Slide the tail into the plane as shown.

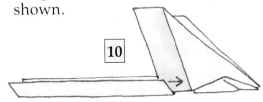

11 Fold down the wings of the plane to make a flat shape. Fold back the front point of the plane and press it firmly into position.

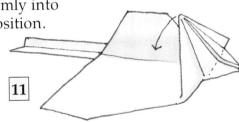

12 Fold up the wings and make a crease halfway down each one.

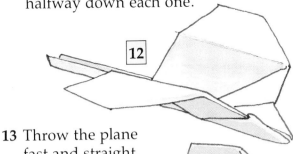

13 Throw the plane fast and straight.

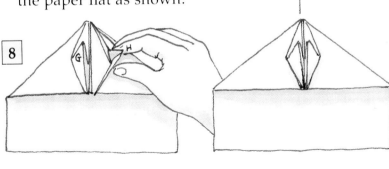

Gliders

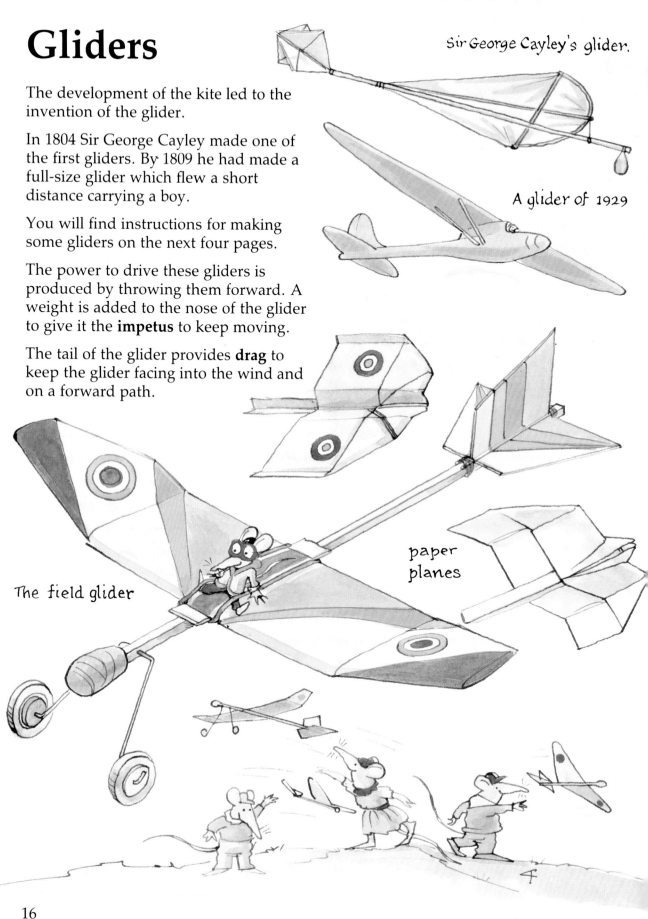

The development of the kite led to the invention of the glider.

In 1804 Sir George Cayley made one of the first gliders. By 1809 he had made a full-size glider which flew a short distance carrying a boy.

You will find instructions for making some gliders on the next four pages.

The power to drive these gliders is produced by throwing them forward. A weight is added to the nose of the glider to give it the **impetus** to keep moving.

The tail of the glider provides **drag** to keep the glider facing into the wind and on a forward path.

Sir George Cayley's glider.

A glider of 1929

paper planes

The field glider

16

Simple gliders

Model A

You will need: an old greetings card about 18 × 14cm (folded), a drinking straw, a used match and some Plasticine.

1 Cut the glider's tail, wings and body in one piece from the folded card. Cut out one **fin** and one pilot from the leftover card. If you have a different sized greetings card, change the size of the pieces slightly.

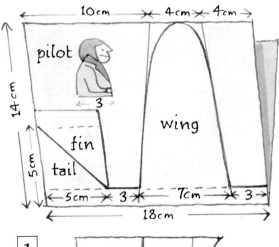

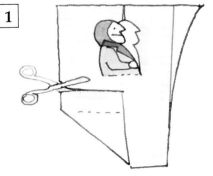

2 Glue the drinking straw inside the fold, positioning the pilot and **fin** as you go. Use small bulldog clips to hold the straw in place until the glue is dry.

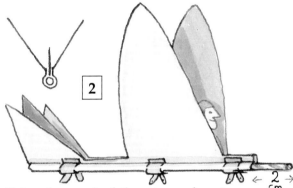

3 Trim the end of the straw, leaving about 2cm to spare at the nose. Push a small lump of Plasticine on to the end of a used match and slide the match into the straw.

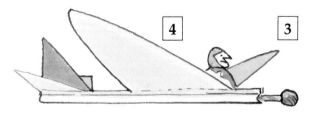

4 Fold down the wings and tail. Throw your glider fast and straight. Adjust the amount of Plasticine to correct any flight problems.

Model B

You will need: thin card about 25 × 7cm, an elastic band, a bendy plastic drinking straw and a nail.

1 Cut the wing and tail shapes from the thin card as shown.

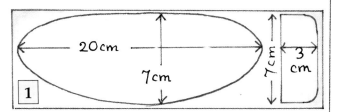

2 Draw a line down the middle of the wing as shown. Do the same for the tail.

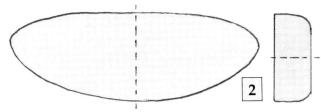

3 Tape the tail on top of the bendy end of the straw.

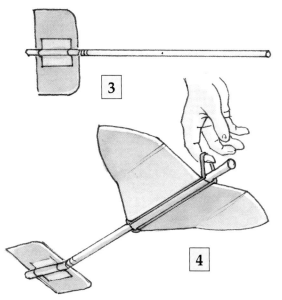

4 Fix the wing to the other end of the straw using the elastic band as shown. The wing will be pulled upwards by the elastic band.

5 Position the wing about 2cm from the end of the straw. Bend the ends of the wings down as shown.

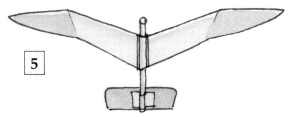

6 Slide the nail into the front end of the straw and tape it in position.

7 Hold the plane by the wing tips to check if it is balanced. The plane should be slightly nose heavy. Bend the straw to alter the position of the **tailplane**.

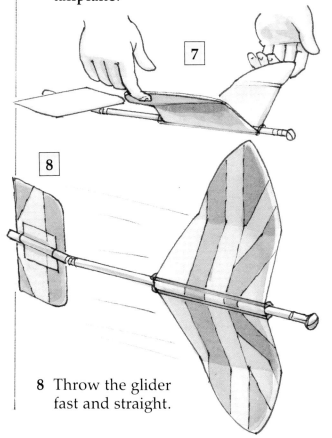

8 Throw the glider fast and straight.

18

A field glider

You will need: 2 lengths of 6 × 6mm square beading, one 50cm and one 30cm, 15 × 3cm of thick card, Plasticine, 2 large and 2 small elastic bands, 25cm of thin wire, 2 identical film can lids, 2 slices of cork about 1cm wide, four pieces of card (one piece 6 × 21cm, one piece 16 × 30cm and two pieces 30 × 21cm) and some used matches.

Paint the glider with waterproof paints. You will find ideas on page 32.

1 Glue the 15 × 3cm piece of thick card to the top of the 50cm length of beading, 10cm from one end. Draw a line across the card as shown. This is the balance line.

2 Drill a small hole through one end of the square beading at A.

3 Push the length of wire through the hole at A so that an equal length sticks out from both sides.

4 Make right-angled bends in both ends of the wire at A and B.

5 Make holes through the centre of the film can lids and the cork slices with an awl.

6 Nail each film can lid to a slice of cork, making sure you match up the holes. These are the wheels.

7 Thread a wheel on to each end of the wire. Bend up the ends of the wire as shown.

The elastic band holds the wheels forward, and takes the shock of a bad landing!

8 Wrap a large elastic band around the top of the wheel unit and body.

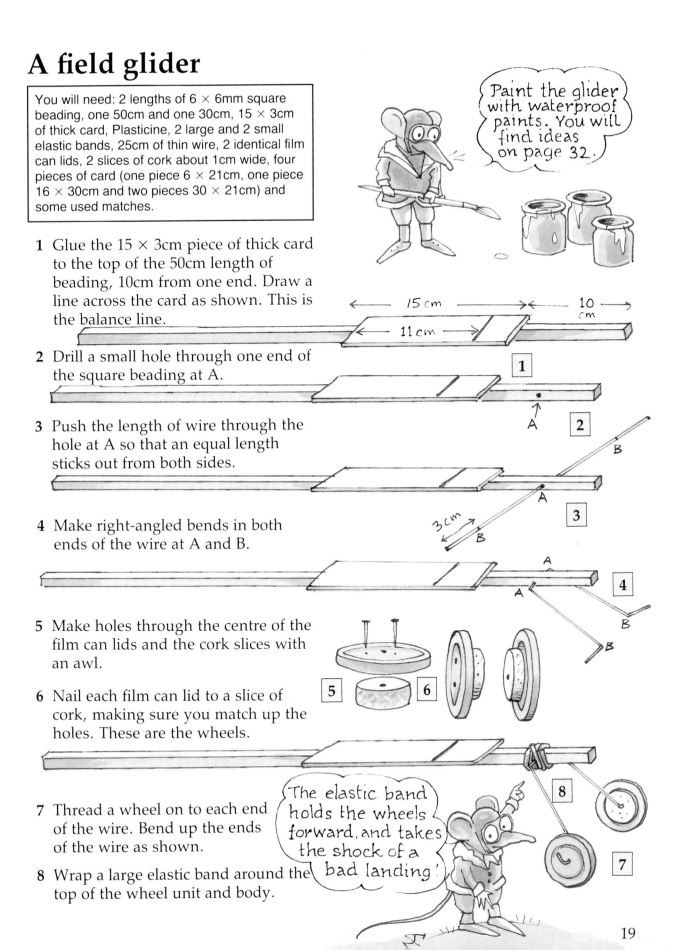

9 To make the tail, cut three **equilateral triangles** each with sides measuring 14cm from the 16 × 30cm piece of card (see page 7). Cut the top off one corner from each of the triangles.

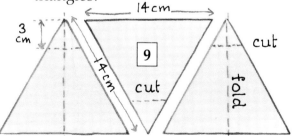

10 Fold two of the triangles in half and glue them together as shown to make a **fin**.

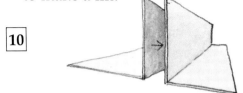

11 Glue the **fin** to the third triangle as shown. Glue and tape used matches along either side of the **fin**, so that they stick out at each end.

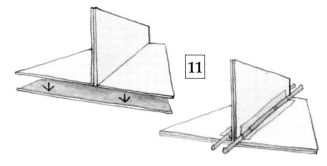

12 Wrap the two small elastic bands around the body and attach the **tailplane** as shown.

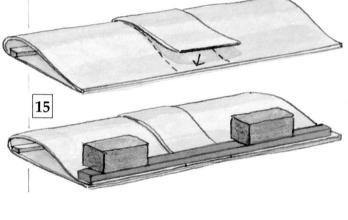

13 To make the wing, draw a line down one of the 30 × 21cm pieces of card, 10cm from one edge. Glue the 30cm length of beading along the 10cm side of the card.

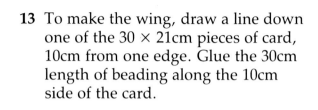

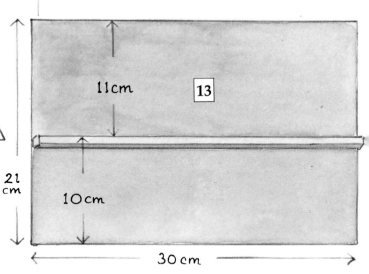

14 Fold the card over and glue and tape the long edges together.

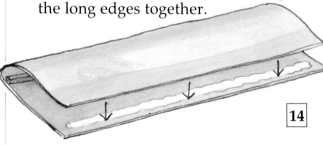

15 Glue the 6 × 21cm piece of card around the centre of the wing for extra strength. Put a weight along the flat edge and leave to dry.

16 To make the wing tips, cut off the corners of the second 30 × 21cm piece of card as shown. Cut the card in half widthways.

17 Fold one piece of card over. Glue and tape sides A and B. Do the same with the other piece of card. These are the wing tips.

18 With the weight still on the wing, spread glue over each end and gently slide the wing tips on to the wing. Support the wing tips with a matchbox at each end and leave to dry. When the wing is set, tape the joins.

19 Hold the glider at the balance line. Add Plasticine to the nose until it balances the tail. Fix the Plasticine in place with sticky tape.

20 Fix the wing to the body with a large elastic band as shown. Slide the wing up and down the body until the glider balances when holding the wing tips. The nose should be pointing down slightly.

21 Throw the glider fast and straight.

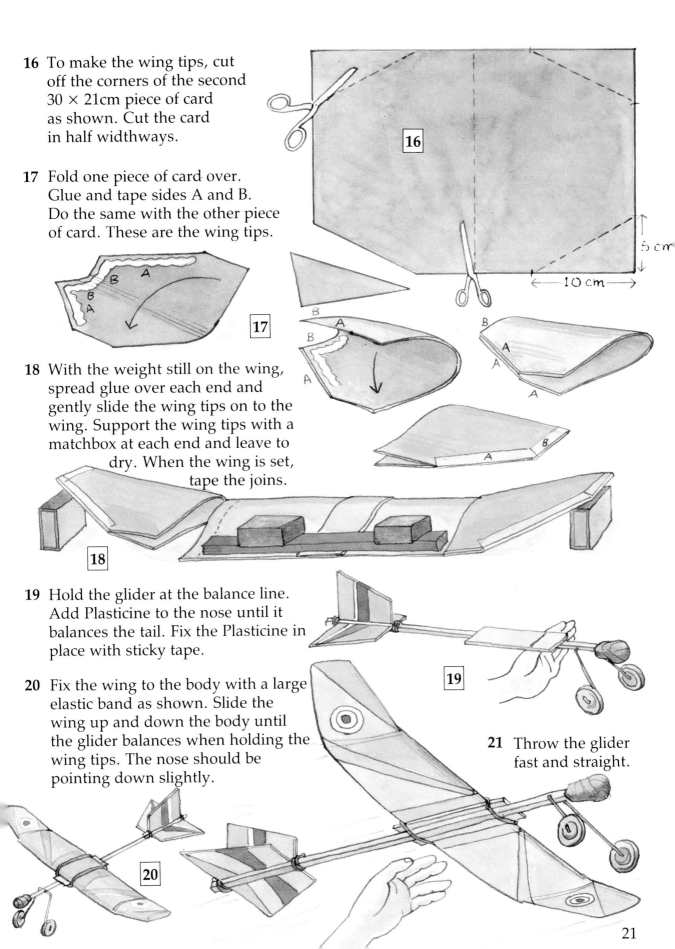

5 cm

10 cm

21

The aerodrome

Build a hangar to keep your aeroplanes in, and a workshop to store all the spare parts.

The workshop

You will need: a shoebox with a lid, a cocktail stick, a piece of tissue paper about 8 × 10cm, a 15cm length of dowel and some thread.

1 Draw two large windows, four small windows and a door on the inside of the shoebox base as shown.

2 Place the shoebox on a block of wood and carefully cut out the windows and door using a craft knife.

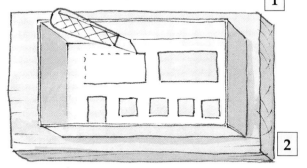

3 Trim the shoebox lid so that it is the same width as the height of the shoebox.

4 Open out the flap at each end of the lid and divide the length of the lid into four equal sections. Mark each section with a dotted line.

5 Make a small cut in both sides of the rim of the lid at A, B and C.

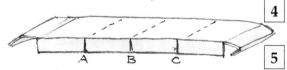

6 Fold the lid along the dotted lines to make two roofs.

7 Glue and tape the roofs to the top of the shoebox.

8 Make a **windsock** from the tissue paper. Tie it to one end of the dowel with thread. Push the other end of the dowel into the workshop.

The hangar

You will need: a strong cardboard vegetable box about 40 × 30 × 15cm, a strong piece of card about 8cm longer and 8cm wider than the box, and corrugated card about 6cm longer than the box but the same width.

1 Cut a large rectangular hole in one of the long sides of the box as shown. The hole should be large enough for your aeroplanes to fit through.

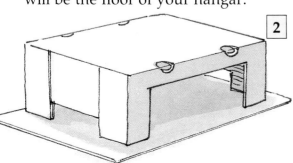

1

2 Turn the box upside down and glue it to the strong piece of card. The card will be the floor of your hangar.

2

3 Cut out the base of the box leaving a 3cm rim all the way round the edge.

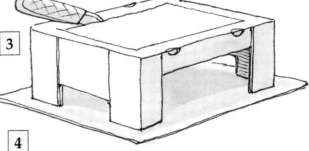

3

4

4 Cut two curved shapes as shown from the card cut from the base of the box.

5 Glue and pin one of the curved shapes on to each long side of the box. Glue the corrugated card across the top of the curves and tape it to each end of the box.

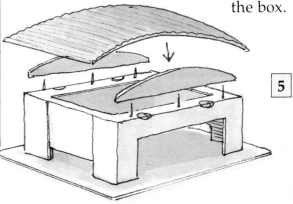

5

Monoplanes, biplanes and triplanes

These models of early planes are too heavy to glide, but you can have fun flying them on a string (see page 25). Keep the flying stick upright. As you swing it round, your aeroplane will rise off the ground with its propeller turning.

You can make the noise of an engine by stretching an elastic band over the top wing. As the aeroplane flies around, the band vibrates and makes a buzzing sound.

You will find instructions for making a **monoplane**, the Gypsy Moth **biplane** and the Red Baron's **triplane** on the next six pages.

The Bristol Monoplane

The de Havilland Gypsy Moth

Flying the aeroplanes

The Red Baron's Triplane

You will need: a stick or cane about 1m long, a nail, 1.5m of strong string, two 10cm lengths of thin wire and a bead.

1 Make a small hole in each end of the lower or middle wing of your aeroplane.

2 Make a small loop at one end of each piece of wire. Attach one of the loops to each end of the string.

3 Tap the nail halfway into the end of the stick or cane with the bead as a washer.

4 Twist the end of one wire loop round the nail so that it swivels freely. Attach the other wire loop to the aeroplane by threading the end of the wire through one of the holes in the wings and twisting the wire around itself to secure it.

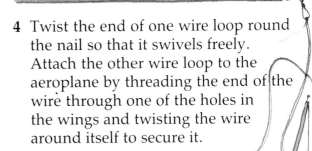

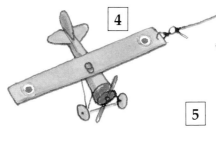

5 Adjust the length of the flying line so that when you hold up the stick, the aeroplane clears the ground.

The Bristol monoplane

You will need: a sweet tube 13 × 2.5cm and two lids, stiff card about 8 × 24cm, a thin strip of wood 23cm long, a cork, a small metal bottle top, 3 thin nails, 2 wire paperclips, a cocktail stick, a thin screw, 3 small beads, a wide elastic band about 14cm long, tin foil about 7 × 7cm, Plasticine, a small piece of wire and pegs and clips.

1 Glue the cork into one end of the sweet tube. Leave it to dry.

2 Cut out a tail and **fin** shape from the stiff card. Slot them together as shown.

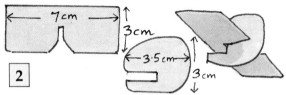

3 Fold in and glue the other end of the tube as shown, sliding the tail into position as you do so. Hold the tail in place with a peg or clip and leave it to dry.

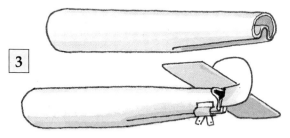

4 To make the wing, draw a line down the centre of the stiff card as shown. Score three lines along one side of this centre line (see page 7).

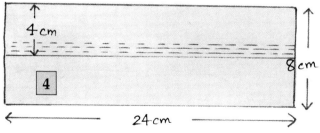

5 Glue the length of wood along the other side of the centre line.

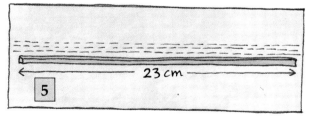

6 Fold the card over the wood along the score lines and glue the sides together. Hold the card in place with small pegs and leave to dry. This is the wing with its **aerofoil** shape.

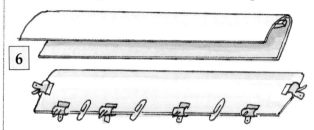

7 Use an awl to make two small holes through the centre of the wing in the positions shown. The holes should be about 2cm apart.

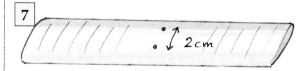

8 To fix the wing to the body, draw a line along the top of the body in line with the **fin**.

9 Use an awl to make two small holes on the line at the front of the body in the positions shown.

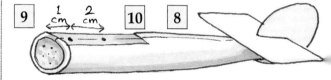

10 Flatten the top of the body a little to make a flat surface for the wing.

11 Glue the wing to the body, matching up the holes in the body with the holes in the wing.

12 Fix the wing into position by screwing the screw into the hole at the front of the wing. Thread two beads on to a nail and push the nail into the other hole in the wing as the pilot's head and neck.

13 Twist a small piece of wire around the nail and screw as the pilot's arms.

14 Cut a propeller shape from the stiff card, cover it with tin foil and pierce the centre.

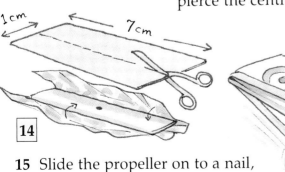

1 cm

7 cm

15 Slide the propeller on to a nail, then slide on a bead.

16 Fill the bottle top with Plasticine. This is the nose. Push the nail through the bottle top and into the cork at the front of the body.

17 Straighten out the two wire paperclips and bend them in half. Bend them around a nail to make a loop as shown. These are the wheel struts.

18 Make four holes under the body and glue in the struts. Thread the cocktail stick through the loops. Make holes in the two sweet tube lids, and glue them on to the ends of the cocktail stick as wheels.

19 Stretch the elastic band under the nose and around the wings so that it rests on the pilot's arms. When you fly the plane, the band will vibrate and make a good engine noise.

buzz!

buzz!

Attach the flying line.

The Gypsy Moth biplane

You will need: a sweet tube 13 × 2.5cm and two lids, a piece of stiff card about 10 × 10cm, 2 pieces of stiff card 23 × 8cm, 2 thin strips of wood 23cm long, 9 cocktail sticks, half a cork with a diameter of 2.5cm, 2 nails, tin foil about 7 × 7cm, some Plasticine, 2 wire paperclips, a bead and pegs and clips.

1 Draw a line down the centre of one of the 23 × 8cm pieces of stiff card as shown.

2 Glue one of the lengths of wood along one side of the central line.

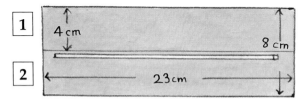

3 Fold the card over as shown, and glue the sides together. Hold the card in place with small pegs and leave to dry. This is the top wing.

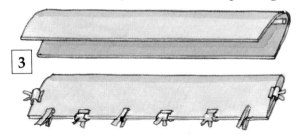

4 Make the bottom wing in the same way.

5 Use an awl or compass point to make eight small holes through the top wing and four holes through the bottom wing in the positions shown.

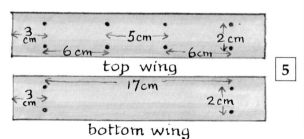

top wing

bottom wing

6 Cut out a tail and **fin** shape from the 10 × 10cm piece of stiff card. Slot them together as shown.

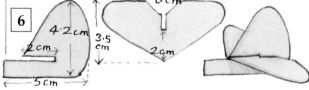

7 Fold in and glue one end of the sweet tube as shown, sliding the tail into position as you do so. Hold the tail in place with a peg and leave it to dry.

8 To make the nose, glue the piece of cork about 3cm inside the other end of the sweet tube.

9 Cut out a "V" shape from one side of the sweet tube as shown.

10 Fill the nose with Plasticine and mould it into a flat shape. Secure the end with sticky tape.

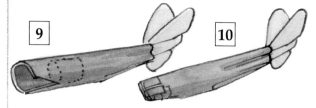

11 Glue and pin the bottom wing to the body. It should be about 3.5cm from the front. Bend the sides of the wing upwards slightly.

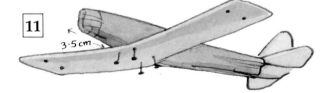

12 Make four holes with an awl in the top of the body in the positions shown.

13 Glue a cocktail stick into each hole in the bottom wing. Slant the sticks forward slightly.

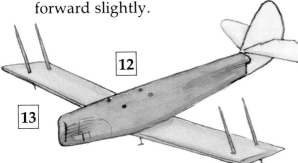

14 Push the free ends of the cocktail sticks up into the four outer holes on the top wing. Glue them into position. The top wing should be slightly in front of the bottom wing.

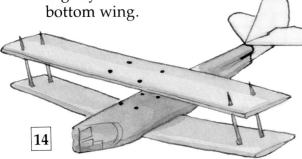

15 Slide a matchbox between the wings at both ends until the glue is dry. The gap between the top and bottom wing should be about 3.5cm. Hold the wings in place with elastic bands until set.

16 Push a cocktail stick through each of the remaining four holes in the top wing and into the four holes in the body. Glue them into position and trim the ends.

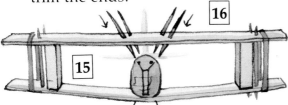

17 Cut a propeller shape from stiff card and cover it with tin foil.

18 Slide the propeller on to a nail, then slide on the bead. Push the nail into the lower part of the nose.

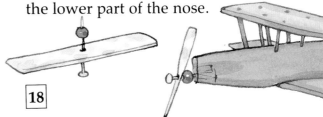

19 Straighten out the two wire paperclips and bend them in half. Bend them around a nail to make two loops, as shown. These are the wheel struts.

20 Take out the pins under the wings and glue the wire struts into the holes. Thread a cocktail stick through the loops. Make holes with an awl in the two sweet tube lids and glue them on as wheels.

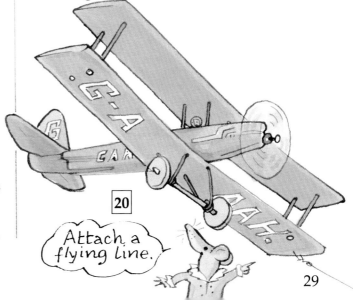

Attach a flying line.

29

The Red Baron's triplane

You will need: a sweet tube 13 × 2.5cm and two lids, 3 pieces of stiff card (card 1, 19 × 6cm, card 2, 17 × 6cm and card 3, 15 × 6cm), a piece of strong card 12 × 5cm, 3 thin strips of dowel (one 17cm, one 15cm and one 13cm), 9 cocktail sticks, a cork, a plastic bottle top, 2 thin nails, tin foil about 7 × 7cm, some Plasticine, a bead and 2 wire paperclips.

1 Draw a line down the centre of card 1 as shown.

2 Glue the 17cm length of dowel along one side of the central line.

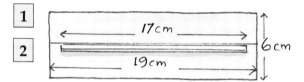

3 Fold the card over as shown, and glue the sides together. Hold the card in place with small pegs and leave to dry. This is the top wing.

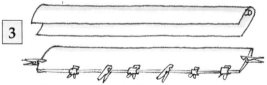

4 Make the middle wing in the same way using card 2 and the 15cm length of dowel.

5 Make the bottom wing using card 3 and the 13cm length of dowel.

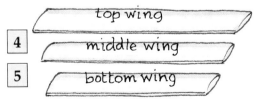

6 Use an awl to make eight small holes through the top wing in the positions shown.

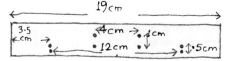

7 Use an awl to make eight small holes through the middle wing in the positions shown and cut out the curved shape.

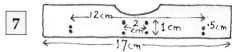

8 Use an awl to make four holes through the bottom wing in the positions shown.

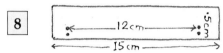

9 Cut out a tail and **fin** shape from the pieces of stiff card. Slot them together as shown.

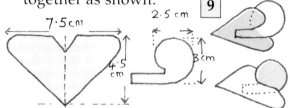

10 Glue the cork into one end of the sweet tube. Fold in and glue the other end of the tube as shown, sliding the tail into position as you do so. Hold the tail in place with a peg and leave it to dry.

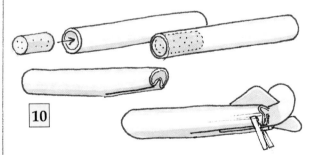

11 Glue and pin the bottom wing to the body. It should be about 2cm from the front.

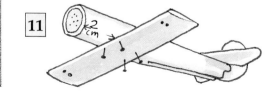

12 Glue a cocktail stick into each hole in the bottom wing. Slant the sticks forward slightly.

13 Wrap a piece of tape around the base of each pair of sticks as shown.

The tape is 2·4 cm wide.

14 Thread the free ends of the cocktail sticks attached to the bottom wing into the four outer holes on the middle wing.

15 Push the wing down so it rests on top of the body and glue and tape it into position.

16 Wrap a piece of tape around each pair of sticks above the middle wing.

17 Glue the free ends of the cocktail sticks attached to the bottom wing up into the four outer holes on the top wing.

18 Push a cocktail stick through each of the remaining four holes in the top wing and into the four holes in the middle wing. Glue them into position and trim the ends.

19 Cut a propeller shape from the stiff card and cover it with tin foil.

20 Slide the propeller on to a nail, then slide on the bead.

21 Fill the bottle top with Plasticine. This is the nose. Push the nail through the bottle top and into the cork at the front of the body.

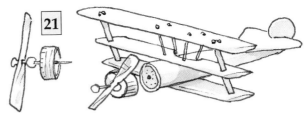

22 Straighten out the two wire paperclips and bend them in half. Bend them around a nail to make two loops. These are the wheel struts.

23 Take out the pins under the wings and glue the wire struts into the holes. Thread a cocktail stick through the loops. Make holes with an awl in the two sweet tube lids and glue them on as wheels.

Attach a flying string.

Decorating your models

Decorating is easier if you paint all over the models with white emulsion paint first.

If you have sticky-backed labels, such as jam jar labels, you can draw the illustration on the label, cut it out, and stick it into place.

If you are flying the paper kites and cardboard gliders outside, it's best to make them waterproof. Either paint the models with emulsion or acrylic paint or finish them with acrylic varnish.

Details of badges, names and numbers can be painted or drawn on with pens.

National markings on early aircraft.

| Great Britain | Germany | France | USA | Italy | Denmark |